William John Fitzgerald

Living in the Shadow of Terror

Spiritual Ways to Cope & Grow

TWENTY-THIRD PUBLICATIONS
A Division of Bayard   MYSTIC, CT 06355

Dedication

This book was inspired by the events of September 11, 2001, and so I dedicate it to the brave—some who went through fire and others who are under fire for the love of their brothers, sisters, and country. And to the hope-filled peacemakers who plant seeds of peace beneath the ashes.

Twenty-Third Publications
A Division of Bayard
185 Willow Street
P.O. Box 180
Mystic, CT 06355
(860) 536-2611
(800) 321-0411
www.twentythirdpublications.com

ISBN:1-58595-205-2
Printed in the U.S.A.

Contents

Introduction

What is behind is the old twentieth century. What is in front of us is a world dramatically changed. This book is framed by the terrors of September 11, 2001. For many years to come, this event will affect the lives of people and nations. Terrorism of many kinds and different origins has now become a weapon used by malcontents. Whether remote or proximate, the shadows of terror are upon us. This book is about coping, hoping, and growing in the shadow of twenty-first-century dangers.

But this book is also about "ordinary dangers" that interface at one time or another with all of our lives. There have always been a variety of terrible moments that intrude and threaten our equanimity. When a woman is told she faces a double mastectomy, for example, or a man is told that his spouse is terminally ill, these are signals of great danger that bring disruption into our lives.

This presence of danger challenges not only our survival skills but also our spirituality because we must depend upon our spiritual moorings when our peaceful lives begin to quake. And so this book suggests strategies for enhancing our spiritual resources, not only in the face of terror and anxiety but in the face of any danger. It also contains prayers of consolation, hope, and courage.

We are all busy people and many folks often make lists of things to

A wise old person is the only one who sees what is in front and what is behind.

■ Homer, *The Odyssey*

do or actions to take in order to provide daily strategies that give order to their lives. There are lists in this book as well. They are not presented as complete or final answers, but they are meant to be starting points for each reader's exploration of his or her own spiritual resources. When we dig deep down into our spiritual resources, we will discover that we are stronger and more resilient than we had imagined. "My strength is sufficient for you," says the Lord. This book is meant to help you call upon the resilient energy that God supplies.

Note that there are journal questions at the end of each chapter. Many people think and pray better when they write out their thoughts and feelings. I invite you to use these questions as starting points for your reflection about how your life has been affected by the events of September 11, 2001.

Following this introduction, I share 12 starting-point disciplines for leading a spiritual life in the shadow of terror. Because I am writing this on October 1, the feast of Thérèse of Lisieux, it occurs to me that there are many "little ways" that we can begin practicing these spiritual disciplines. St. Thérèse felt called to focus on "little ways" of loving and serving God in her daily life. May she be our guide along this path.

12 Disciplines for Living Spiritually

1. Cope with danger or any intermittent terror by opening yourself up to compassion, not closing down with fear.

2. Be awake! Be aware of more than just danger. Let your heightened sensibilities be more alert to beauty all around you and the precious gift of family and friends. Keep your priorities straight.

3. Search for meaning in the gospel message of Jesus.

4. Believe and reaffirm daily that love is ultimately more powerful than hate. Realize that in the short run striking back may achieve results, but in the long run only love and justice can bring peace. As Pope Paul VI said, "If you want peace, work for justice."

5. Widen your spiritual horizons by acting for social justice in the global village. Learn to reduce anxiety through discipline that is holistic and healing.

6. Learn to reduce anxiety through spiritual disciplines like prayer and meditation. Life today has too much anxiety and stress. Since September 11, this has been magnified.

7. Most of us will never encounter a terrorist, but everyone at one time or another will encounter a terrible disease or accident. Terrible things do happen to good people. Our spiritual response must be based on our firm belief and immersion in the paschal mystery of the life, death, and resurrection of Jesus.

8. Pray prayers of serenity, protection, and courage.

9. Let new challenges call forth the best of your inner qualities. Cope by not letting the threat of danger take control of your thinking, your heart, your feelings. If the threat of terrorism holds your feelings captive, they win. Rather, let these challenges call forth your faith, hope, and love—the best resources to nourish your spirit.

10. Deepen your spirituality. Learn that the basic flow of all creation is from chaos to order. At the deepest levels of matter, creation is ultimately relational and interdependent. In your spiritual life pay more attention to deeper reality than to what is trivial and on the surface.

11. Listen to what the children and young people in your life are feeling, and share with them how to be vigilant but not anxious.

12. Fast, conserve, and simplify as important elements of your spiritual life. Be proactive against terror by widening your spiritual concerns toward the poor, the hungry, the marginalized. Always believe that the power of Jesus Christ surpasses that of evil. Evil has its moments but we can cope and hope because we firmly believe that "The ages belong to Christ."

These spiritual disciplines will be elaborated upon throughout the pages of this book.

Falling

So high! So mighty! Falling, Falling into rubble!
Horror!
September 11, 2001

U.S.S. Oklahoma and our world
Upside down! Infamy!
December 7, 1941

A nation torn and severed
Brother against brother
1865

The Roman God—Mars
levels the Holy City
March, 70 A.D.

Where is God?
Is our God silent?

one

Coping

Be strong and courageous. Do not be terrified; do not be discouraged, for the Lord your God will be with you wherever you go. ■ Joshua 1:9

From the beginning of time people have had to cope with terror in some form or another. Consider the Middle Ages, for example. Cities all over Europe were surrounded by walls for protection against barbarian raids. In the fourteenth century, people were terrorized by the Black Death. And the church sang, "Dies irae, dies illa!"—"day of terror, day of wrath." Those were the worst of times, but every century has had its share of terror. And yet history teaches us that our ancestors coped and hoped and passed on to us the good news of the gospel.

The Shadow of Terror

The Hebrews have wept and wailed in the rubble of the temple for 2000 years. The difference in the new century in North America is that we thought it could never happen here. Beyond our tears and fears, we must cope and hope, for we too now live in the shadow of terror, either remote or proximate, as we search for God in twenty-first-century rubble.

The poet Richard Eberhart, writing about the horror of a twentieth-century aerial bombardment, remarked on God's apparent silence and how mankind continues to kill as Cain did. People are "no farther advanced than in their ancient furies." He writes further that the infinite spaces are still silent. It is that way with horror. It arrives with clamorous fury and noise and then—only shocked silence. We are left to ask, "Where is God? How can we cope?"

But after the first long, shocking silence—God does begin to speak. It happened on September 11, 2001 and in other times and places of horror. Our God is a God of love, not terror. And God speaks through us when we lay down our lives for our neighbor. The footsteps of the fireman rushing up the steps of the leaning inferno were the footsteps of God. The sounds of the rescuer's footsteps were the sound of Christ's footsteps as he plodded step by step up the hill to Calvary.

A few days after the towering inferno in New York, a local fireman appeared at my door and asked if he could have a moment of my time. I welcomed him and he held out his hand and asked if I would bless his medal of Saint Florian, patron of firefighters.

After he left, I realized that he is the one who gives me a blessing each and every day, and someday he may even give his life for me. Through such as these God speaks.

The Offspring of Terror

Terror generates its own offspring; their names are revenge, hate, and despair. They are as old as time and they knock at our door with clubs. Other children of terror are named grief, compassion, help, resilience, coping, and they are old too—but for the followers of Christ they are born anew—"Anno Domini," in the year of our Lord. When terror abandons and dumps its offspring upon us it is for us to us to choose which we shall adopt. Which of these children of terror do we want to bring into our homes and mingle with our own children? This is a question that the new twenty-first-century terror asks all of us. And our faith challenges us with another question, "How are we to live spiritual lives in the shadow and aftermath of terror?"

In Easter Week, 1916, a band led mostly by teachers and poets rose up and seized the General Post Office in Dublin, Ireland. There was a siege and the rising was quashed. Later, after seeing the leaders of the uprising being led out of the rubble and many of them executed, the poet William Butler Yeats realized that out of their suffering a new nation would be born. In his words, "a terrible beauty is born!"

In our own time and place we have experienced our own rubble—in Oklahoma City, in New York City, in Washington, D.C., and countless other places in our individual lives. Tragedy transcends time and place, though. It belongs to all of us and is shared by all of us as a people, a nation. Now is a new time. And a new time needs a new nation. Out of our own terrible rubble, a terrible beauty is born. The "terrible beauty" is the tremendous compassion born of tragedy.

The last survivor pulled from the wreckage of the World Trade Center described descending the steps hand in hand with a coworker. Then the world around them collapsed. Hand in hand, they fell through space and in a moment they were thrown apart and she landed wedged between concrete and steel. She would be entombed there for twenty-seven hours. In those hours she prayed and tapped. And then the hand of a fireman reached down through the rubble and touched hers. A terrible beauty!

Reaching Out with Compassion
This is an image that might well inform and inspire our own spiritual lives—reaching down—reaching out in compassion. We are all in this together now—this new world of ours—a world where we sometimes live in the shadow of greater danger. "You cannot come after me, unless you take up your cross daily." This is our cross now—to occasionally live in the shadow of terror—but with our hands linked together in compassion. We can cope because we reach down and reach out in compassion.

And after the smoke, and the fire, and the confusion on September

11—this is what happened. This event moved the whole country into a new space, a new mood. Deep compassion stirred the hearts of a nation. A terrible beauty!

The last decade of the twentieth century was not so much epitomized by compassion as it was with self-gratification and self-satisfaction. Everything was going up for a lot of people—salaries, the stock market, affluence and abundance. In the midst of affluence, it is easier not to be conscious of our dependence on other human beings or even of God. When the twin towers fell, it shook the very foundation and self-preoccupation of the nation. I am reminded of the little glass balls that would hold a winter scene and would be given as Christmas gifts. They would only become fully beautiful when you shook them up. When turned upside down and shaken and then turned upright again, a beautiful winter scene would appear, with little snowflakes filtering down on the scene below. That is what happened on September 11, 2001. Our whole world was turned upside down and shaken. And out of that horrible shaking, there came a terrible beauty.

People seem a littler kinder, a little more gentle, a little more patient with each other. Of course, toward the terrorists there was a righteous, energizing anger—but for the victims and their loved ones—the deepest compassion. People came together. We no longer thought of "those brash New Yorkers who think the world ends at the Hudson River." Nor did New Yorkers think of "those hicks out in Iowa." No, we began to think of ourselves as Americans, as brothers and sisters together in a great venture of healing.

Politicians who too often over the last ten years of the old century were engaged in so much rancor and pettiness, stood together under hard hats at the ruins of the towers and the Pentagon. Though their hats were hard, their hearts were softened. And what they had too often neglected through partisan bickering became a priority again—the common good. And the simple things of life—family, neighbors, connections—became dear and all important again. Yes, in the smoking ashes, a terrible beauty was born. It will be our challenge in the new century not to forget that beauty, but to enhance it.

Creeping Terror

Terror sometimes comes with fury and thunder. At other times it may creep into our lives on cats' feet. Terrorists provide a vivid frame for the portraits of danger that hang in the galleries of all of our lives. Danger can come from many sources. It can come from the skies or in terrible accidents on life's crossroads or through economic slumps, or it can come ever so quietly within the bodies of our loved ones as their cells are invaded by disease. We all stand at a crossroads. One road sign points in the direction of retreat. The "Retreat Road Sign" leads us in the direction of panic or even unremitting anguish and perhaps bitterness or despair. The other road sign that says "Compassion" leads down the road to helping and encouraging. It is the path of comradeship and love. Each one helps the other, saying, "Take courage!" No matter what the danger or tragedy, when we walk this path of compassion together, we are connected. We need not fear. It is the path of the Lord.

> You, O Lord, are the everlasting God,
> the Creator of the ends of the earth.
> You do not faint or grow weary;
> your understanding is unsearchable.
> You give power to the faint,
> and strengthen the powerless.
> Even youths will faint and be weary.
> and the young will fall exhausted;
> but those who wait for the Lord
> shall renew their strength,
> they shall mount up with
> wings like eagles,
> they shall run and not be weary,
> they shall walk and not faint.
> Each one helps the other,
> saying to one another, "Take courage!"
>
> ■ Isaiah 40:28–31; 44:6

Journal Questions

- As I reflect on the 12 spiritual disciplines on pages 6-7, which do I find the most thought-provoking?
- Which do I most need in my life right now?
- What effect have the events of September 11 had on me?
- How has my life changed?

Fear: The Bit Player

There is nothing wrong with fear.
It is one of the players in the drama of our lives.
We should accept fear as an actor, but never
*   give it the lead role.*
For no great drama was ever successful with fear
*   as the main actor.*
And yet, some fear must be present in any great drama.
Fear looked over the shoulder of Jesus in the garden,
But it did not stop his mission.
Fear accompanied Peter as he walked on the water,
But it did not stop him from launching out...
Fear accompanied the martyrs against the lions,
But it did not destroy their faith and hope.
Fear accompanied Washington as he crossed the freezing
*   Delaware,*
But it did not row the boat.
Fear rode with Lincoln on the road to Gettysburg
But it did not stop his speech.

Fear is a like a nervous actor who always wants
*   the lead role.*
Never give fear the major role.
Never give fear more power than it deserves.
Let fear have a minor role, some lines, but not all.
Give fear lines of caution, but not panic,
lines of deliberation, but not inaction,
lines of prudence, but not cowardice,
lines of discernment, but not foolhardiness.
In your own drama of life,
Fear deserves no more than a bit part.
Give faith, hope, and love
the leading role.

two

Hoping

Hope does not disappoint us, because God's love has been poured into our hearts by the Holy Spirit that has been given to us. ■ Romans 5:5

The story of terror is an old, old one and it erupts at various times in the whole order of creation, both in large and in small ways. In the human realm it can interrupt our lives at any age. When I was growing up, I lived in a wonderful neighborhood where there were lots of kids. In a very real sense, we were a community. We played together, went to church and school together, and the neighborhood was a safe place to live together.

Of course, as we grow our peripheries expand. We journey out of the safe and the predictable. I was just a skinny little kid and I recall at age 7 or 8 walking to school and sometimes being joined by another kid, not from the neighborhood, who was three or four years older. He would walk alongside me and suddenly my world was not safe because he taunted me and pushed me around. As I remember it now, my main strategy was to cope by distracting him with questions about other things and to talk to him as if he were one of my neighborhood friends. And this strategy often worked. Nevertheless he really was a bully. In some micro-degree, all bullies are terrorists! How I responded as a child was a psychological, intuitive, and, indeed, a spiritual strategy. I acted as though he were my friend! My first effort at diplomacy.

Most parents know that their children will encounter bullies. It is part of the game of life. So my father taught me to box and defend myself, but when you don't have the weight to put behind a punch, that defense can be futile. I remember another time when I was in the seventh grade when a kid started harassing me on the playground. The feeling of being harassed is a terrible feeling. Somehow or other, I managed to get into close quarters with him and grabbed him. We were on concrete in the schoolyard. I managed to get a bear hug on him and then by some magic of the moment he was caught off balance and he went crashing down on the cement. Not a smooth landing. I have never seen anyone so startled in my life. He gave me a good stare and then walked away. I was as surprised as he was.

In those years the sisters talked a lot about guardian angels. Perhaps the same angel that wrestled with Jacob was on my side. The only other experience I had with bullies was as a freshman in high school. A kid from another class was taunting me, and one of my classmates, a Sicilian American with dark eyes, gave this kid the stare and told him to lay off. It worked. (He is a bishop now—no, not the bully—the Sicilian American with the dark flashing eyes!)

As children, we learn certain strategies to deal with bullies. First we cope and that gives us pause to hope. We may try diplomacy—talking our way out. It is always a good first step. Sometimes the diplomacy and hoping has to be followed with some kind of action. This is true whether the bully is just annoying or potentially lethal. Coping, hoping, acting will very often diminish the power of bullies.

The Theme of "The Bully"

Bullies are often depicted in literature and films. The very fine movie *Hearts in Atlantis* will be on the rental shelves for a long time because it addresses this theme in a wise and hopeful way. In this film, the marvelous actor Anthony Hopkins becomes a mentor for a ten-year-old fatherless boy played by Anton Yelchin. Anthony Hopkins himself is being pursued by vague faceless characters who fit the definition of bullies. So are Anton and his neighborhood friend, Mika Boorem. When three older schoolyard bullies confront Anton and Mika, two hold Anton and the largest of the three bullies grabs at Mika's undeveloped breasts and mocks her. She weeps tears of fear. This is bullying advanced to a higher degree than I had ever experienced. At that moment, Anthony Hopkins appears and confronts the leader of the bullies. He stares at the boy and reveals the secret weaknesses and proclivities of the bully and the bully deflates in front of him and skulks away.

This is a terrifying scene, for it is an undeserved confrontation. The aggressor holds the upper hand and tries to humiliate and control the boy and the girl. This is a subtle form of terrorism! And at the moment the girl is touched and mocked, real terror is present.

Kathryn Scheckel, a real-life girl, the same age as Mika, wrote a poem about "fear" as a bully. She called it: "Dial 1-800-HOPE"

> Fear is like a constant bully.
> It makes you feel scared and confused.
> You feel alone and don't know who to turn to...
> You are so caught up in fear you forget your priorities:
> Fear of losing family,
> Fear of dying,
> Fear of Terrorists,
> Fear for your future.
> These seem impossible not to fear,
> But hope can help you fight fear.
> Hope is fear's worst enemy.
> You can always depend on hope.
> Hope conquers fear.

In some way children's bully scenarios might be seen as the image that prefigures spousal abuse. Little bullies grow up to be big ones and it is no longer the little girl on the street, it becomes the derogatory "little woman" of the household. This kind of terror can be as close to any of us as the house next door.

All of these examples are pretty tame compared to today's modern street gangs with automatic weapons. In these cases these youth are usually powerless youngsters with no futures, no hope. One of the reasons they terrorize is because it is the only way they can exert power. They are impotent in every other way. Bullying and terrorizing are all about control. For some, their terrorizing is the one island of "order" for themselves since they live in a totally chaotic environment. Terrorism has many potential seeds often sown in youth and bearing bitter fruit in teen years and young adulthood. It is the same for international terrorists—seeds of hate, revenge, envy, or religious fanaticism are planted long before they step on the terrorist stage and act out their inner fury.

Chaos and Order
The story of bullying is an old, old story going back to Cain and Abel, and David and Goliath. Goliath thought by simply staring at the young David, he would terrorize him. He was wrong. David coped. David hoped. David prevailed. Chaos turned into order. There have been many Cains and a lot of them in some ways resemble the bully in the movie *Hearts in Atlantis*. Hitler was a failed artist. Mussolini was a stupid fellow who covered up his shallowness with bluff and bravado. Emptiness sometimes invites in the furies. Osama bin Laden has been described as a model child but a very unhappy and frustrated one. Each of these men achieved "success" as bullies. The paradox is that they themselves saw their enemies as bullies. Hitler labeled the Jews as financial bullies. Mussolini invaded the weak country of Ethiopia, bragging that it was a powerful opponent. He built an arch of triumph to celebrate his great victory. His troops shot cannons at natives with bows and arrows!

Terror, too, has been around a long time. The Romans crucified victims not only to kill them but to strike terror in the eyes of the beholders. And, after the Civil War, the bullies of the Ku Klux Klan, cowards

behind masks, burned fiery crosses not out of any devotion to the Savior
but to terrorize and subjugate blacks. Such perpetrators achieved their
own "order" by bringing chaos to those around them. The blacks had to
cope to survive—but also to hope for change. Black leaders emerged to
give hope to their people to stand up to the bullies. Their strategy was the
firm conviction that hope and love are more powerful than hate. Martin
Luther King once said, "We must meet hate with creative love."

Hope nourishes love, and love is creative. Hate nourishes terror and
terror is destructive. When we look at the various manifestations of bullying, in the short term, self-defense and even retaliation have often succeeded in stopping them. However, in the long term, hope and creative
love have been much more effective in stunting bully growth. Armed
forces had to stop Hitler in the short term. In the long term, the Marshall
Plan fulfilled the gospel command to love even your enemies. It gave
hope to Europe. General George Marshall, after waging war, sowed the
seeds of future peace.

Martin Luther King and Gandhi also believed that, in the long run,
nonviolence would ultimately be more powerful than violence. And
each of them succeeded in reaching their goals. All three of these men,
to one degree or another, were influenced by the radical teachings of
Jesus about loving your enemies.

Question Arising from Terror

In our own time, terror, especially in its most hideous eruptions,
throws a penultimate question into our faces. When we consider the
gas ovens of Auschwitz, the rubble of the great towers of New York, the
thirty-one million Russians among all the others who perished under
communism and in the two world wars of the twentieth century, are we
not tempted to ask if there is something fundamentally corrupt at the
core of humanity? Could it be that this inner corruption impels
humanity on a downward slide into ultimate annihilation? There really is no hope for improvement because the human is fatally flawed.
Terror challenges us with such questions.

For Christians, these are not new questions. After the Black Death,
and countless wars and destruction, at the time of the Reformation in
the sixteenth century, Christian theologians debated the very question

about the human core being corrupt. One school held that human nature was in essence corrupt and had to be covered over by the redeeming Christ. Another held that human nature was wounded and needed healing by Christ. Yes, at birth, human nature is wounded by sin, but never totally corrupted.

Wounds can heal. It is the belief in wounded human nature that moved Father Flanagan, the founder of the original Boys Town, to proclaim, "There is no such thing as a bad boy!" Where there is the possibility of healing there is hope.

What are the powers of the spirit that arm us with hope? How do we cope with the ancient mystery of human evil? For one thing, we need to reflect on stories of hope in our own communities—like Jesse Smith's. Jesse is a young black man from New York who in his younger days had no place to sleep but on the subway. He was hospitalized for gunshot wounds. As a drug dealer, Jesse got shot by a fifteen-year-old whose only reason for not killing Jesse was that he ran out of bullets. As he said himself, he had always dreamed of helping youth and here he was, pushing drugs to them instead.

Jesse Smith lived in a world of terror and shadows. He soon became #46191, sentenced to 4 to 6 years in prison. He admits prison was painful. He says he lost everything except not giving up on himself. After prison, he moved to Omaha to join his mother. In Omaha, a Federal Enterprise Zone had been set up to redevelop intra-city infrastructure and develop jobs—a creative effort to restore hope. As a part of this program, Catholic Charities hired forty individuals from impoverished areas to work on building a drug treatment center. Jesse was one of them.

Out of this experience a local business, Vaughn Electric, gave Jesse a further chance by hiring him. After three years, Jesse finished his electrician-training classes. Now he is on his way to becoming a journeyman electrician. He still wants to restore hope in the hearts of other inner-city kids. "If I can get youngsters to see what I've been through, maybe they won't have to go to prison. I've been through too much not to share." There are "Jesse Stories" all around us. They are all about becoming proactive and finding hope in the midst of chaos. Jesse lives close to Girls and Boys Town where there are countless stories of young men and women who have been terribly wounded by chaos—but not totally corrupted. Their wounds are healed because Father Flanagan believed that no child at the very core is corrupt or evil, only wounded by evil.

Hope and Love? or Hate and Terror?

If the penultimate question in the shadow of terrorism is: "Is human nature fatally flawed?" then perhaps the ultimate question is: "Which is more powerful: hate and terror or hope and love?" This is a spiritual question for all past ages and especially for our new century where terror has become sophisticated and elusive, clever and devastating. In our age, the devil does go about like a roaring lion seeking those he can devour. Demonic power does devastate. And until the end times, so long as humans possess free will, humans will have to have firm hope—and be proactive against terror. The most powerful arms we have for this struggle are our faith, hope, and love, which place Christ at our side in the best of times and the worst of times. Satan always cringes before his footsteps. Satan does have his moments. But Christ is the Alpha and the Omega—the victorious "Lord of All the Ages." Thus we have hope for all the ages.

And when the shadow times come, with Christ at our side, panic or fear need not overtake us. If we allow that to happen, the terrorist and the bully win. They have control of our inner spirits. In this context consider the following quotes.

If God is for us, who is against us?… Who will separate us from the love of Christ? Will hardship or distress, or persecution or famine, or nakedness or peril? or a sword? No, in all these things, we are more than conquerors through him who loved us. For I am convinced that neither death, nor life, nor angels, nor rulers, nor things present, nor things to come, nor anything else in all creation, will be able to separate us from the love of God in Christ Jesus our Lord. ■ Romans 8:31–39

We have nothing to fear but fear itself. ■ Franklin Roosevelt

Over and over the gospels are filled with the message the angel gave to Mary: "Do not be afraid!" And this humble maiden did not cower even in the face of the terrorist Herod. She coped. She hoped. And she and Joseph acted to protect their child.

None of us can ever avoid terror completely. Is not cancer a terrorist who viciously attacks? Is not Alzheimer's a terrible affliction? We know that there is conflict close at hand for everyone, and whether germs come to us through a sneeze spreading dangerous flu, or a biological attack, we are mortal. But we need not live dead lives shadowed over by fear. "The coward dies a thousand deaths, the hero only one." And so in the best of times and the worst of times, we wait in joyful hope for the second coming of our savior Jesus Christ. But in our waiting his ever present Spirit sustains us.

What terror has done is wake us up from complacency, from taking each day for granted. Iraeneus said that the glory of God is the human fully alive. Terror alerts us not just to danger but to life! Cherish each dawn. Live each day as if it were to be your last, as indeed one day it shall. Be a messenger of hope in what you say and do. Bring the power of love into all your dealings. Conduct business justly. Have concern for the poor around us and around the world. Do that and you are being proactive against all terrorism.

As we wait, we do indeed need stories of hope and courage and we find these in the actions of those who risk and sometimes give their lives to save others threatened by tragedy or terror. We also find them in the stories of the lives of the great saints. Let them guide us. They stood face to face against the roaring, demonic lion. It breathed flames against the maiden Joan of Arc. She stood strong and courageous. So did Maximilian Kolbe who volunteered to take the place of a condemned father of children at the doors of the Auschwitz ovens. And it was so for all the holy martyrs. Their names and their spirits continue to soar while their oppressors are dust in the dust bins of history.

Journal Questions

- Right now in my life what will help me to cope?
- Whose example inspires me most at this time in my life?
- In what ways have I been an example for others in the face of terror?
- Do I live each day as if it were my last?

Hope Comes Alive

But hope is not hope if its object is seen. How is it possible for one to hope for what he sees? And hoping for what we cannot see means awaiting it with patient endurance. Romans 8:24–25

At the end of the old century,
our lives were cocooned in certainty.
Advertising was our assurance of perfection.
We could purchase everything.
And the market went up, up and away.
We grew satisfied and complacent.
Life was on an aimed trajectory.
We had our eye on our target.
And we were in complete control.
We had conquered the moon
and were on our way to Mars.
When certainty prevails
hope wanes.
What more is there to hope for?

The new century ushered in uncertainty,
and thus an opportunity for hope to thrive.
Hope comes alive when we are not sure,
when we encounter doubts and fears.
It is then that we need hope.
And she comes always valiant
to walk by our side.
Hope does not flourish
on the brightest day.
Hope comes alive
on the darkest of nights.

three

Meaning

The riddle and insight of biblical faith is the awareness that only anguish leads to life, only grieving leads to joy, and only embracing endings permits new beginnings.

■ Walter Brueggeman, *The Prophetic Imagination*

In 1999, at the pre-dawn of the new millennium, a United States customs agent stopped a car at Port Angeles, Washington. She found the look in the eyes of the driver to be dead. "His eyes were dead," she said. When the car was searched, there were enough chemical materials to produce a massive explosion. And so the great celebration of the new millennium went on—kept safe by one observant lady who noticed dead eyes. Confetti fell in the canyons of New York and the Space Needle stood secure.

Too soon in the new years of the twenty-first century, not confetti, but debris and smoke and fumes would fall down like lava from hell. It is a new century. It is in so many ways a new world. Things are not the same in this new century as they were in the old. It is a world of endings and new beginnings. Some things are better. Some things are worse. Terror around the world, of one kind or another, like a fierce bear, will slink back into its cave and sleep, but it will not sleep forever.

We realize that not all terror comes from terrorists. There are terrible events that result from accidents, from storms, from illness, from children shooting children. In some form, at some time, each individual who lives will face something terrible. How these encounters can be meaningful is one of the most searching questions faced by human beings. People will search in many places for the answer. As Christians we are challenged to search the gospel for meaning.

The Search for Meaning
Adolph Hitler wrote a textbook of terror in blood's ink and in burned flesh in his concentration camps. He was a pioneer in organized, well-thought out, well-planned terror. And he made it look good! After all, the Gestapo wore well-tailored black and silver uniforms. It was only the poor wretches in the camps who looked bad. No wonder we pray in the renewal of baptismal promises, "Yes! We reject the glamour of evil!" There is a certain fascination with terror—at least in the movies and on TV—but fascination evaporates when it is seen up close and real.

A story is told of a concentration camp inmate and it went something like this. He was found kneeling and praying. "What are you praying about?" He responded, "I am giving thanks." "For what?" "That I am not the one in the tower with the power to shoot you and me." One of the great writers who survived the concentration camps said that what sustained him and others was that even in the worst of circumstances their lives had meaning. His name was Viktor Frankl. He wrote that neither power nor prestige were at the core of the human quest. The search for meaning was the deepest human need.

"What is the meaning of all of this?" This is a question that surfaces whenever we have to deal with terrible happenings. Not all terror originates with terrorists. Fate is a constant theme of literature. This is exemplified in the novel *The Bridge of San Luis Rey*. Why did some perish and others not? In our own lives and experience, we all encounter terrible situations where some survive and others perish. Why some and not others?—we are moved to ask.

I pick up this morning's paper. Two school buses made their way back from a happy event. One goes over the side of a bridge. One stops. Some live. Some die. Why? What is the meaning of all of this? I remember 40 years ago, driving back from a football game with five high school students packed in the car. The radio was blasting with loud music. You could not hear any other sound. We drove through a little town where the train passed only once a week. We never heard a whistle. As we got our front wheels onto the track, the whole interior of our car was illuminated with brilliant light from a train's headlight. It was yards away and bearing down on us. We made it over the tracks by a few feet. What was the meaning of such a close scare? What did we learn? Well, we all learned that life can be very chancy. Sometimes the line between tragedy and safety is only a few feet or even inches.

In the larger scale of things, terrible tragedies teach us that every life is an adventure. No one is ever totally secure. Before this new century, all of our ancestors lived in proximity to danger. Over recent years we have become complacent living in a safe zone. No more. Danger is closer. And danger tests us. Like gold that is tried in the furnace, we too are tested and refined through danger, tragedy, and turmoil. The meaning that we discover in terrible circumstances can vary from person to person. For the prisoners in the concentration camp observing the guard with the gun, the meaning was, "I am really in a better position than he is. He is a hollow man with a gun that he may have to use in some cruel way. I do not. I need not be cruel. I do not have to be like him or my other oppressors. They are hollow men for whom life is cheap."

Viktor Frankl could stand up to his oppressors because life meant something to him. It meant little to the men with the guns. He would write later that when a person finds it their destiny to suffer, that is their own unique task. In his book, *Man's Search For Meaning*, Frankl wrote, "His or her unique opportunity lies in the way in which he or she bears the burden." He calls this testing of the spirit a "unique opportunity!"

The students in the car lit up by the train's headlights may have learned that they were not immortal. Consequently, they could better appreciate the things that perhaps they took for granted. After crossing that railroad track, I learned that life can take sudden unexpected turns. None of us is ever in complete control of every situation. Part of the mystery of life is that there is a certain randomness in the course of human events. But it is also true that chaos and turmoil test us to our depths. Think of the variety of responses we can give to horrible events. We might cower in fear. We might rush in to rescue others. We might become angry and bitter. We might reflect and learn. We might become hateful and withdraw. We might become more generous and helpful. Or such events may be triggers to anxiety or depression. Researchers estimate that nearly eighteen million people in the USA suffer from chronic depression in normal times. That figure surely increases in the aftermath of terrible events.

In order to be guided by hope and courage, we must at some deep level come to see chaos as an opportunity to grow rather than as a hindrance. The human spirit that refuses to be shackled sees meaningful opportunity even in the midst of chaos.

If life is seen as a journey rather than a refuge in a safe house, we will possess the energy to cope with messiness and move through chaos. Messiness is almost a daily given—traffic jams, missed deadlines, family arguments, unpleasant coworkers—and it often leads to chaos. To deal with chaos, we must have a resolute spirit and wells of fortitude to move through and out of it. It is never an easy passage, but it is a necessary one. As the old adage proclaims, "If you are going through hell, whatever you do, don't stop!"

In the old century the best human qualities were tested by the chaos of war. When World War II was over, the returning vets had discovered meaning in their efforts. And when old folks talk about those chaotic days they will say, "We lived through the war." At the end of that war, world peace had been established, democracy secured, and the evils of Nazi and Japan's warlords' terror smashed. Because of victory, there were many meaningful memories for those who had experienced the crucible of terror and destruction.

On the other had, so many vets returned from Vietnam feeling that all their sacrifices went unacknowledged and in the end had been in vain. Too many had lost a sense of meaning and carried with them the terror of nightmares. I know a wonderful, well-educated, mentally healthy, and productive member of society who served on a helicopter gunship in Vietnam. He still occasionally has Vietnam nightmares, but he has succeeded in building a life with meaning in spite of lingering memories of terror. Many others are unable to cope. One sociologist has theorized that the majority of the homeless men on the streets are Vietnam vets!

How We Grow Strong

Suppose there was no chaos. Suppose life was never messy. Suppose we lived in an antiseptic world. Would we grow if life never tested us? As human beings we are wired for growth either upward or downward—to be either fulfilled by love or to be diminished by hate. "Fulfilled"—what does this word mean? It presumes that there are empty spaces within us. Being fulfilled means more than just filling our stomachs. It means finding meaning through rising to the occasions when life tests us to the extreme.

The firemen rushing up the steps of burning buildings to rescue others and subsequently perishing—were their lives fulfilled? Yes, in one terrifying moment. Of course, their loss was an enormous grief and diminishment for their families. But is it not also true that spouses and children who saw them leave "for work" daily as ordinary people now glimpsed them and appreciated them in an even deeper way when they reflected on their finest and last hour? They know in a very painful way the magnificent valor of their loved ones. And they now know that all the "I love you" words spoken through the years by those firefighters have an even deeper and more profound meaning. For some life can be finally menacingly fulfilled in a few moments. For others it takes a long time.

The young man who, in the terrorist attacks of September 11, led the charge of the passengers on a hijacked airliner, died too soon by our human reckoning—in the prime of his life—but also he died at the apex of generosity. In all these examples, the efforts of "ordinary people" accomplished deep and meaningful results. It has always been so for those who lay down their lives lovingly for their friends.

Once upon a time, there was a young man who died way too early.

He was truly human and he never knew the warmth of wife and family. In fact, he had no real home. The foxes have dens, he said, but he had nowhere to lay his head. He was seized by terrorists and his friends deserted him. He was too young to die. He had no children. He had no grandchildren. He was falsely accused. He was spat upon and reviled. He was unjustly condemned. And so the Roman terrorists decided to make a spectacle of him. They drove nails in his hands and feet and hanged him between two outlaws to die. Jesus of Nazareth was put to death by terrorists. And when all was said and done, his disciples were left to ask the question, as people always ask after every tragedy: "What does all this mean?"

The Road To Emmaus
This was the question asked by the two disciples on the road to Emmaus following the terrible events of Good Friday. They were hightailing it out of town. They thought they had been deceived. They could not wait to put miles between themselves and the events of the previous Friday. But then a stranger joined them. Their eyes were downcast and they did not recognize him. All they could see was the camel dung spread along the road. They began to bemoan the disaster that had occurred and how they had hoped that this Jesus would be the messiah. It was only in their telling of the story that they could search for meaning. The stranger at their side helped them to discover the real meaning of the events they mourned. And finally as they sat down to eat, they recognized Jesus "in the breaking of the bread." They discovered after all that the events of Good Friday were not empty and hopeless but rather full of meaning.

We Possess Good News
Terrible things do happen to good people. Terrorists do prowl across the pages of history. Those who nailed Jesus of Nazareth to a cross were among the very worst. Down through the centuries civilization has only managed with great effort to put a thin veneer over savagery. Indeed its seeds still lurk within all of us. However, through all of that the gospel has continued to be good news. It contains the mystery of

the suffering servant who has passed through the worst terror and who can lead us through it as well. So who are we? We are people who possess good news even in the midst of the worst news.

Terrible things have always happened to good people. We would wish it otherwise but its presence is woven into the fabric of our lives. It exists in the micro-world too. There is a constant battle going on within each of us between micro-invaders—cancer, pneumonia, plague, and AIDS. In some sense these diseases are like terrorists who advance on our defenses to struggle with the immune soldiers that guard our lives. And when such invaders enter the lives of our loved ones and conquer, it is a terrible thing.

So how do we stand against this kind of terror that keeps stalking about and plotting strategies to defeat us? As the followers of the crucified and risen Jesus, we are the disciples on our own road to Emmaus. It is only on that journey that we can find the deepest meaning for our lives. It is contained within the gospel and the paschal mystery of Christ's life, death, and resurrection. We too know the joy of success and the misery of failure. We too would prefer that everything go right. But everything does not. We too experience the messiness of the camel dung on the road. We too know the heights of love and the depths of rejection. Our lives are complicated. Our road is not straight and level. Sometimes we lose our way and go off the road into a ditch. And we often struggle back. It is precisely in our struggles that we discover who we are. Our lives are a mystery and we do not know the ultimate ending, but we do have the assurance of an ultimate destiny. Our life stories are woven into the paschal mystery—the life, death, and resurrection of Jesus Christ.

The Ultimate Test

Perhaps the ultimate test of meaning for all of us is whether we can still love God and others in the midst of tragedies, terrors, misfortunes, and suffering. Jesus seems to be telling us that it is precisely our ability to love in the very worst of circumstances that brings us the deepest meaning for our lives. "Where your treasure is there is your heart." Think for a moment, if we were never loved, or if we never loved, what treasure could take the place of such an emptiness? Nothing.

Alzheimer's is one of the worst terrors for those who must deal with it. It is a stealthy terrorist that sneaks up slowly. And it is all the more terrible when it creeps upon a loved one or a lifelong mate. For it slowly sprays a toxic cloud of not knowing, not remembering, not responding over someone with whom we would want to share our dearest memories. Once upon a time, at a seaside retreat house, I met an elderly man whose wife had disappeared in a cloud of unknowing. He was her caretaker, and he had taken time out for a weekend retreat, where he might re-group and decide his next step. He had reached a point where he needed outside help. This help was necessary because he had been waking every two hours of the night to check on his wife, lest she

Journal Questions

- What does "I love you" mean in my life right now?
- What terrors have I faced and triumphed over?
- In what ways has my faith in Jesus Christ helped me to deal with messiness and chaos?
- What has given the most meaning to my life up to now?

wander away. His night-long waking was his fulfillment of that first "I love you" spoken so many years before. As I sat later by the shore, I reflected on what "I love you" really means. And I concluded that here was a man whose life was full of meaning for he had lived through the heights and depths of the journey of Christ. His love from early courting to caretaking had run a full course. For some, fulfillment can come in an instant through some heroic act. For this old man, fulfillment required a long twilight vigil.

For now, at the end of his days, he was living out the full meaning of those youthful words, "in sickness and in health," that he had promised so long ago. Yes. Here was to be found the fullest and final meaning of love.

What "I love you!" Means

I met love today, not in a song, not in a movie, not in a book,
no, Chuck walked in and said: "Can I eat with you?"
Chuck, seventy-two years young,
coming to be renewed, apart to a quiet place.
Chuck, married fifty years, is now a caretaker,
his wife with Alzheimer's, lost.
Chuck has a "safe room" where she can walk at night,
and do no harm to room or self.
He arises every two hours to make sure,
to keep watch, to keep faithful
to that "I love you!" whispered shyly half a century ago.
Then, pulsing with young stallion's blood,
He could not know, nor could he guess
that she, a willow full of promise, would someday be his cross,
his bittersweet cross, in that safe room,
a fulfillment of that first "I love you."
Two young lovers clamber up the rocks from the sea below.
She is windswept and wet,
her shirt clinging to her body proclaiming:
"I am ripe and full of promise!"
Go talk to Chuck, climber of the rocks!
Learn from him what "I love you" means.
And then find a lover who half a century from now
will look at sunken sockets
with as much fondness as now your lovely breasts evoke.
Your lover, now in his virile youth, holds your hand
as you walk along the rocky ledge.
There is strength, security, surefootedness,
as the waves break below.
But for greater courage, deeper meaning, go to Chuck's house,
to a safe room, and meet love waking every other hour.

four

Learning

Question: "Will Russia be the biggest threat to peace in the future?" Answer: "No, we have successfully avoided war with Russia. No, in the future the greatest threats will come from radical Middle Eastern fundamentalists, or perhaps from the Mafia being able to deliver a nuclear weapon in a suitcase."

■ former Secretary of State Dean Rusk, 1986

In the twentieth century our questioning was about the nuclear threat from Russia. In the Cuban Missile Crisis, we lived with the sword of Damocles trembling over our heads. The Russian question is no longer asked. In the new century, our questions are more concerned with scattered terrorists dispersed in many lands. This new century has opened up entirely new chapters in the history of war and peace. In the previous century, the United States was involved in six wars: the First World War, the Second World War, the Korean War, the Vietnam War, the Gulf War, and the conflict in Yugoslavia. In all of these conflicts no casualties occurred on North American soil. In the new century, thousands of military and civilian casualties have been suffered right here in our homeland. In this chapter, I will look at nine questions that have arisen from the ashes of September 11. They are twenty-first-century queries.

Question One

How can people who claim to be religious promote and carry out terrorism? If we search for the roots of religious intolerance we will find fundamentalism deep in the hearts of many religious persons. We all know religious fundamentalists. Some are Protestant. Some are Catholic. Some are Muslim. Most of the ones we know are probably well-intentioned and kind. They live side by side with us in peace. They may or may not be involved in evangelistic efforts to convert others to their denomination or spirituality. However, there are others who carry fundamentalism to its most shadowy extreme. In some sense, they put God in a box—in their container—and refuse to believe that God can even be found beyond just their categories. Thus their reasoning would go this way:

> Our God is the true God. Since we possess the true God and you are different from us in your belief, you do not possess the full truth or the true God. God and salvation are on our side, not yours. You need to be converted to our belief to be saved. You are infidels if you do not worship our true God. Consequently—your worship of God is false. It follows then that your version of God is a threat to ours. Since your views threaten us who are the bearers of God's truth on this earth, if you were to spread your false beliefs this would be harmful to our truths. Thus your threatening beliefs must be eradicated in order to safeguard our true beliefs. Since we are holy and you are not, if this cannot be done by persuasion, it must be done by force.

This sort of thinking is what psychologists describe as "projection"—projecting one's own hidden evil on those who differ. Jesus described this as seeing the speck in someone else's eye and not noticing the beam in one's own. It should be noted that angry terrorists really "hijack religion" for their justification and cover. It becomes an alibi for their rage, some of which is recent and some that is ancient. This "hijacking of religion" has been pointed out by Tony Blair, Prime Minister of Great Britain. He proclaims that there is no such thing as a genuine "religious terrorist," for all terrorists of any stripe reject all religion in its best and truest sense, while at the same time they use it as a tool to promote their agendas.

Question Two

Why would anyone call Americans "The Great Satan"? If someone, Osama bin Laden, for example, believes that his religious way of life is the only true way, and if others claim "truths" that to him seem to be the opposite, he sees his own views as "light" and sees opposite views as "darkness." If forces of light and forces of darkness are led by Satan, the opponents of bin Laden, the bearer of truth must then be Satan's agent. This is religious fundamentalism at its most basic. Virulent fundamentalism draws a line between those who have the "right" God and those who do not. And if they do not possess God, they are with Satan. This way of believing is simplistic but very appealing, especially to uneducated people, some of whom have no personal experience allowing them to interact with those "outside their own camp."

Question Three

Who are the enemies of the various terrorists scattered around the world? Their enemies are those governments or groups who in their view promote injustice, or who may be authoritarian and suppress their grievances, or any government or agency that threatens their culture or religion. Usually their direct enemies are not armies. Rather, their basic enemy is the ideology they consider unjust or opposed to their prevailing culture. Therefore, their most effective weapon is terror against civilians. Where there are democracies, terrorism against the populace is most effective because it can affect the activities of democratic governments who depend on citizen support.

Question Four

Are we ourselves ever justified in using terrorism as a weapon? We have done so. We used weapons of mass destruction when we ended World War II by dropping atomic bombs on Hiroshima and Nagasaki, Japan. We did not drop those bombs to destroy military targets. Nor did we drop them in revenge to vaporize innocents. Our purpose in using weapons of mass destruction was to terrorize the civilian populace and their rulers and thus end the war. It worked. We justified using these weapons of terror because it would quickly end the war and in the long run cause fewer casualties than an invasion.

Question Five

Why might terrorists target our American culture and our presence in the world? American culture is exported everywhere through film, TV, books, etc. It is threatening precisely because it is so pervasive. Some people in the world do not want to be like us; they reject our materialistic and secular values. They want their children to grow up in a religious culture. People who have never known Americans judge them to be like what our video and film images portray. One aspect seldom portrayed is the deep religious and spiritual values held by so many Americans. Instead, we are seen as totally secular with little value given to religion.

Through television, in particular, the poor and demoralized people of the world see Americans as violent, arrogant, wealthy, and godless. Though many Americans are deeply religious, not much of that comes through. Our television image is the only one that many poor people around the world see, and most of them have never met an American. There are of course "ugly Americans." Consider this message "Bad American" that is circulating on the internet even as I write this. It sums up what many people think of Americans and it's not a pretty picture.

> I'm a Bad American. This pretty much sums it up for me. I like big trucks, big boats, big houses, and, naturally, pretty women. I don't care about appearing compassionate. I don't think being in a minority makes you noble or victimized. I have the right not to be tolerant of others because they are different, weird or make me mad.

This is my life to live, and not necessarily up to the expectations of others. I don't want to eat or drink anything with the words "light" or "fat-free" on the package. I don't believe in hate-crime legislation. Even suggesting it makes me mad. Don't tell me that someone who is a minority, gay, disabled, another nationality, or otherwise different from the mainstream of this country has more value as a human being than I do as a white male. Yes, I'm a bad American and proud of it!

Question Six

How can we learn more about what breeds terrorism? We can learn more about the breeding grounds of terrorists by learning more about the injustices that sustain them. The fact is that some terrorists are highly motivated and believe they act in a just cause. If they were on our side and were sacrificing themselves to preserve an America direly threatened, we might consider them heroes!

Question Seven

When we live in the shadow of terrorism, either looming or remote, how should we pray? We need to pray prayers of trust in God's care. Many of the psalms express this trust beautifully. We need prayers of hope. We need prayers of solidarity with other persons of our own faith and of other faiths as well. Ecumenism should have a rebirth. Vatican II, in the "Decree on the Relation of the Church to Non-Christian Religions," tells us to reject nothing that is true and holy in other faiths. Several years ago, Pope John Paul set a beautiful example for us by going to Assisi to pray in a spirit of tolerance and cooperation with a wide variety of believers, Christians as well as Jews, Buddhists, and Muslims.

Question Eight

If we are to love our enemies, what are the spiritual resources we need to draw upon? We must deepen our faith, our hope, and our love by living not just for ourselves, but for others as well. We must love our neighbors as ourselves and that means all our neighbors far and wide. A spirituality that is concerned only with personal salvation isolates us from the pain and struggles of people around the world, including our enemies. How can we possibly love those who hate us? We need to pray for them. That perhaps is the bottom line for followers of Jesus Christ. We also need to pray that their grievances of our enemies, if justified, will be heard and addressed.

An important way to show our compassion for others—even our enemies—is by supporting groups and organizations such as Bread for the World, Catholic Relief Services, or Amnesty International. These organizations, and many others like them, work for justice and bring compassion to those who are suffering worldwide.

Question Nine

How can we be proactive? Both Vatican II and the social justice teachings of recent popes provide a wonderful rationale for being proactive against terror. In their document "The Church in the Modern World," the council fathers of Vatican II declared that "the joys and hopes, the grief and the anxieties of the people of any age, especially those who are poor or afflicted, are the joys and hopes of the followers of Christ." They proclaimed that the social order must be founded on truth, built on justice, and animated by love. Thus social justice and the common good are prerequisites for maintaining peace in the world.

Perhaps the most dramatic proclamation of this rationale was from Pope Paul VI at the United Nations. There he proclaimed to the nations: "If you want peace, work for justice!" Pope John XXIII and Pope John Paul II have also called for justice in our dealings with others. They alert us to the fact that there is indeed great injustice in our world. When people are victims of injustice, poverty, and violence, there exists a breeding ground for war and terror. Though many of the international terrorists are not poor, part of their agenda is to stir up resentment among the powerless against those who are perceived to exploit and endanger them.

The fact that two recent popes have addressed the United Nations and that the Vatican is represented there should also alert Catholics that the UN is deserving of our support and not our scorn. "If you want peace, work for justice!" So what can we do as individuals? We can support national policies that seek social justice for the poor in our own land and in the world. Groups like Network, Bread for the World, and the Campaign for Human Development actively work to this end.

To be concerned about the children of the "global village" is to plant seeds of peace for the future of our own children and grandchildren. As Mahatma Gandhi said, "If we are to reach real peace in this world, and if we are to carry on a real war against war, we shall have to begin with children."

Journal Questions
- How much do I know about other world religions?
- Do I ever pray for my enemies? Why or why not?
- What is my reaction to "Bad American"?
- In what ways am I concerned about the "global village"?

Our Mother Earth

She holds us and she feeds us.
Seldom do we look at her.
How rarely we touch her.
She weeps. She groans. She trembles.
Yet when she is wounded,
We are wounded too.
She is stripped, poisoned, abused.
Yet she labors forth life.
Her gift is our birth.
The Pope kisses her.
She is whence we all came.
And to whom we all go.
She is our Mother, the Earth.
She is ours. We are hers.

The Human Spirit craves depth
at its deepest core,
meaning and fulfillment.
The Human Spirit can be
muffled by noise,
trivialities, and baubles.
The Human Spirit
is embodied—with a right to food
for body and spirit.
The Human Spirit yearns
to move with deeper purpose.
It is elastic, stretching out.
The Human Sprit is snapped,
twisted, and depraved by hate.
But the Human Spirit
is indomitable—
because it is empowered
by Love.

five

Deepening

Significantly, the most gripping religious symbol or quasi-religious spatial image to appear in recent decades is the photograph of a fragile, spherical planet earth viewed from a space capsule. The viewer however is not looking up but looking down...modern pilgrims are more affected by depth than height.

■Harvey Cox, *In The Presence of the Sacred Room*

To live spiritual lives in the shadow of danger, our worldview and our spirituality need to deepen and widen. At the close of the old century, our culture was obsessed with the trivial and the material. That is never enough to satisfy the longing of the human heart and certainly it is not enough in the twenty-first century. Now we need to deepen our faith, our hope in the future, and our love for our sisters and brothers around the world. We also need to look beyond the surface of world events to see some of the underlying causes of turmoil and anger. We need a deeper spirituality, one that is unifying, connective, and peacemaking. We need to go deeper and wider in our social-spiritual concerns. Our spirituality is now lived out in a global village. I became convinced of this when I myself began to see the world through a different lens.

A Deeper Journey

Some years ago, I was in Jordan preparing to cross the border into Israel the next day. That evening in the hotel I was approached by an Arab who identified me as a Christian. He said his brother, a Christian, was in Bethlehem and would I be willing to take a message about some television sets over the border with me. I saw no reason not to, but then he surprised me by saying he would hide the message in a box of candy and his brother would take it from me after crossing the border. In my naivete I said okay.

I was also carrying with me a suitcase filled with clothes for a friend who was studying in Jerusalem. When I arrived at the Allenby Bridge, the entry to Israel, I experienced Israeli security. When I told the border guards that I did not have the key to my friend's suitcase, of course they took it apart and unfolded every item within. Then with my plastic sack containing the box of candy in hand, I was ushered toward a shower-like stall for a body search. My hands now felt a little clammy, holding the sack containing the box of candy with its hidden message. As I entered the stall to undergo a complete body scan, I simply put the sack on a shelf next to me. Amazingly, they never looked into the sack. Israeli security, the tightest in the world, scanned the surface but never looked into the sack! The moral of the story: surface obsession can distract from grasping the hidden essentials. As soon as I crossed the border, an Arab appeared from nowhere and took the sack uttering many thanks.

That set the tone for the rest of the journey. At that time there was peace on the surface, and yet there were Israeli soldiers everywhere with Uzis hanging from their shoulders. And when I looked into the eyes of

Palestinians, I knew there was no real peace. When I saw their eyes I was reminded of what my father had told me almost forty years before. "As long as the displaced Palestinians remain in squalid refugee camps, there shall never be peace." Some of them are still there.

The Journey Into Egypt

After traveling to all the holy places, from Galilee to Jerusalem and Jericho, we embarked on the longest leg of our journey—across the desert on our way to Egypt. This experience would take us back through all the centuries. Out on those desert wastes, there were black Bedouin tents no different from the tents of the ancients. Some had tumbleweed pens tied with string to corral their scraggly goats. We were traversing both in geography and in time into a different world.

Eventually we crossed the Suez Canal where Muslim workers paused from their labors to kneel and face Mecca, bowing in prayer. When we came to the Nile, it was like a step back into the day of the Pharaohs. For here were people living as poorly and primitively as they did when the Hebrew people pitched their tents here and worked at hard labor.

A City of Contrasts

When we entered Cairo, it was like no city I have ever seen—swarming, exotic, timeless, a city of contrasts. The five-story houses of the dead stood silent, block upon block, and below them the clamor and squalor and dust were rising from the footsteps of thousands of people. The contrasts were so extreme: the ancient Pyramids swarming with tourists, high-rise tourist hotels surrounded by teeming throngs of Egyptian people. You might drive down a street and follow a long string of camels who followed a Mercedes. Here again, the contrast between rich and poor demanded observation.

After showering and enjoying the creature comforts of a modern and comfortable hotel, I wanted to visit the Coptic Christian Church of the Flight into Egypt. To get there, I had to leave our modern hotel and walk through the squalid tenements that are off the beaten track. Here again, I was given a glimpse of what lies beneath the surface, something tourists rarely see.

Cairo is representative of the Middle East in so many ways: the contrast between rich and poor, the vast numbers of people, most of them poor, and a young population that continues to swell. Like other Muslim countries, it is held together by an authoritarian regime. And beneath the surface, there are swelling resentments.

For the last half of the old century, the whole Middle East has resembled a powder keg with a smoldering wick. And it is here that America has pitched its tent. The United States has no troops in Paraguay. Why not? There is no oil there. The Middle East has been volatile, remains volatile, and there is every reason to believe that it will remain volatile in the years ahead. It is important that we look below the surface there and understand some of the differences between east and west. "East is east and west is west and never the twain shall meet" is an old saying that no longer applies. We have met and we must understand.

The vast teeming numbers of people on Cairo's streets reminded me that 80% of the people living in the world, a majority, do not share the same values as Americans. What we take for granted as "reality" is not their reality. The Middle East's highest value is honor and their greatest affliction is shame. Our highest value (judging by the media) is success. In the east, patriarchy reigns supreme, and family bonding and ties are sacred. If you strike one brother, you strike all. Thus, the most extreme group in Egypt is named "The Brotherhood."

The pot stirring in the Middle East mixes religious fundamentalism, dire poverty, restless youth, and resentment against the western military presence. Military actions against Middle Eastern countries are seen as assaults on the "brotherhood." This is what always simmers and brews below the surface.

We Need To Get Connected

How to be connected is a lesson we might learn from the east—but here again we need to look beneath the surface. The very fabric of our civilization is threatened; we need to re-connect at the deepest level of reality. The connectedness of the quantum world and a recognition of the possibilities for peacemaking can take us deeper and make us wiser. When we delve deep enough, we discover that the basic flow of all creation is from chaos to order. At the deepest levels of matter, creation is ultimately relational and interdependent. There is no rugged individualism at the quantum level. In some sense the deeper we go into matter, the more we realize that everything is connected. This realization should have practical consequences for believers. It reveals a wisdom imprinted by the creator on the very fabric of reality.

The Ground of Being

Paul Tillich described God as the "ground of being." Thomas Merton once wrote that if you descend into the depths of your own spirit and arrive somewhere near the center, you discover that at the root of your existence you are in contact with the infinite power of God. This center is beneath the ego. And the passage to the center is a path of letting go of selfishness. Thomas Leach in *Soul Friend: The Practice of Christian Spirituality*, describes this journey of prayer as taking us from the superficial and false self into the deepest and real self.

God is deep down beneath all else and this deep down presence underlies our spiritual journey, which is to be through intermittent chaos toward order. In fact, the chaos/order dichotomy is not really real. The flow toward unity underlies even all chaos. Consequently to be religious in the deepest sense means that we connect at a deep level no matter what our different surfaces tell us about our differences.

Our hearts are made for the deepest of all realities. They are made for treasure that is even deeper than the depths of the quantum world. The underlying essence of reality, which unites us all, is that mysterious presence we may call by different names, but most commonly call "The One God." Saint Augustine wrote that our hearts are made for God and restless till we rest in God. It is this presence that all human hearts seek, whether they be Muslims, Christians, or others. Thomas Merton in *Contemplative Prayer* describes this deepest reality as: "The Abyss of the unknown yet present—one who is 'more intimate to us than we are to ourselves!'" It is there that we will find our peace and unity.

Christians and War

War is the result of prejudice and misunderstanding. We know that throughout the history of Christianity our ancestors have sometimes justified chaos rather than peacemaking, disconnection rather than connection, and division rather than unity. How many wars have been fought (and are still being fought) over religion? It is important that we look deeply into war and see how the Christian response to it has evolved.

There are two streams of theology within the Christian tradition regarding the justification for waging war. The oldest and narrowest stream starts with Roman soldiers who found conflict with teachings of Jesus and military service. Origen, an early prominent Christian theologian, taught that fighting in any war contradicted the teachings of Jesus. Saint Francis of Assisi also opposed war, and in more recent centuries, Mennonites and Quakers have opposed war, as did Dorothy Day (her Catholic Worker followers are pacifists as well).

The far wider stream of Christians who find justification for war starts with Saint Augustine in the fourth century who developed a theology of a "just war." Through the centuries the majority of Christians have drunk from this stream, and most wars right up to our own time have been justified based on this just war theology, which states that war must have a just cause, avoid direct harm to civilians, be motivated not by hate but a desire to stop aggression, and what is to be gained must outweigh harms that can reasonably be foreseen. Richard McBrien, reflecting on recent history, states that if there ever was a war that met these criteria, it was the war against Hitler, and he adds that the twenty-first-century war against terrorism also meets them. This majority of Christians who justify waging war are closest to the words of Augustine. It seems to me that those who put the sword away are closest to the words of Jesus. If for no other reason, it would be wise for me and the many other Christians who justify some wars to at least honor and respect the dissenters.

Perhaps the result of the convergence of these two streams of theology will be the realization that bombs, guns, and war can only be stopgap measures. The deeper truth is that only peacemaking can ensure peace. Quantum physics reveals that everything is interconnected. If seeds of hatred and revenge are planted, war is seeded and will eventually reap a bitter harvest. If proactive love, compassion, and justice are planted, seeds will more likely reap a harvest of peace. Two great generals of World War II started as warmakers and ended as peacemakers. Toward the end of his long and brilliant military career, General of the Armies Douglas MacArthur would write:

In the evolution of civilization, if it is to survive, all men and women cannot fail eventually to adopt Gandhi's belief that the process of mass applications of force to resolve contentious issues is fundamentally not only wrong, but contains within itself the germs of self-destruction.

As a conqueror of Japan, instead of wreaking vengeance, MacArthur built democracy and allowed the Japanese at the same time to retain their emperor as a figurehead. His counterpart, General Marshall, became Secretary of State and helped initiate the Marshall Plan, which rescued and built up our former enemies, the Germans. It is one of the great humanitarian efforts of all times. Enemies were turned to friends and allies. MacArthur and Marshall planted the seeds of peace in the old century and the harvest is still being reaped in our twenty-first century.

Seeds of Conflict

After World War I, the opposite happened. The Treaty of Versailles attempted to humiliate the Germans and turn their industrial areas into pasture. At least some of the causes of World War II were seeds planted by this harsh treaty. Although the causes of all wars are complex, it is not too farfetched to show that there is a string of connections: in the aftermath of World War I and the Treaty of Versailles, Germany lay prostrate. The Great Depression proved fertile ground for Hitler's rise to power. When in power, Hitler junked the treaty and rebuilt Germany into a world power. He needed a scapegoat and picked the Jews. This resulted in the terrible holocaust. After the Second World War, the Jewish people needed a homeland. The United Nations intended to carve out a Jewish homeland in Palestine and a separate Palestinian homeland. Israel preempted this by occupying 77% of the territory and Egypt and Jordan the rest. In a subsequent war, Egypt and Jordan were expelled. Two of the great peacemakers were assassinated by terrorists—Anwar Sadat, the Egyptian leader, and Yitzhak Rabin, the Jewish leader. On and on it has gone, and there are still hostilities. Bitter seeds yield bitter fruits. When will we ever learn? When will we ever learn?

If we want peace, we must deepen our vision and plant the seeds of justice, compassion, and love!

A Global Village Spirituality

Joseph Moore, writing in "Plough" and surveying the spiritual climate in the USA at the beginning of the new century, wrote these provocative words: "Our fundamental sickness remains: our society is essentially organized selfishness on a grand scale."

Is this too harsh? Some of the spiritual literature at the turn of the century would seem to reinforce this. So much has been written about securing God's blessings for ourselves. If we follow the right prescriptions, we will progress and know the blessings of prosperity. There are many spiritual books that purport to show us just how this can happen for believers. Wayne Dyer writes that we must "manifest our destiny." *The Book of Jabez* by Bruce Wilkinson urges us to "widen our boundaries." So much of American popular spirituality is about ME using the right techniques—and often the payoff will be "prosperity" given to us by God.

To be "spiritual" means much more than selfish concern for our salvation and our prosperity. To be spiritual in the new century means to live in a global village where we are all connected in the web of life. It means to "love our neighbor as ourselves" and to act for the common good. Instead of asking personal questions like, "Am I saved?" or "How can I be blessed with God's prosperity?" there are these deeper and more challenging questions:

• Who is my neighbor? (Jesus was asked this question. It remains our question.)

• Since all people of the world share limited resources, what can we do to be less selfish in their use and more conserving of Earth's bounty?

• What can we do to help the poorest of the poor to help themselves?

• How much Third World debt can and should be forgiven?

• What can we do about the 35,000 children around the world who die every day from hunger, war, AIDS, and lack of medical resources?

If we move from trivial surface concerns to the deeper things that matter, we will recognize our freedoms as seminal and essential. However, our freedoms are also our most potential weakness because those who would terrorize us can wage war against all citizens and thus in their view sway public opinion. That can and has backfired before. However, the real Achilles heel of democracy is when large numbers of citizens fail to participate by ignoring issues and failing to vote. This weakens our greatest strength, the very muscle of democracy.

The Bible does not tell us how to vote, nor should religious leaders. However basic biblical injunctions should lead us to try to find the course of action or the political persons who will do the most for the common good, at home and around the world, not the person who will do the most good for special interests. Not to vote is to abandon the very roots of democracy. If we do not vote, why should others—sometimes with their lives—defend our freedom to do so?

When we see the view of planet earth from space we cannot see Muslims, Protestants, or Catholics. This view of reality ought to convince people of all denominations that we are one human family living together on this one blue and green planet. From this viewpoint, divisiveness and religious intolerance seem so foolish. As mentioned earlier, in 1986 leaders of all the major religions gathered in Assisi, the city of Saint Francis, and prayed together for peace and unity. Pope John Paul has called for yet another such gathering in 2002. Surely whatever we personally do to continue ecumenism and interreligious dialogue will plant the seeds of peace. Prayer can change the world!

Journal Questions

- In what ways do I need to deepen my understanding of the global village?
- If God is "the ground of being," what does this mean for the human community?
- What is my own theological stand toward war?
- How do I personally answer the question, "Who is my neighbor?"

What Rises from the Ashes of War?

Force can overcome resistance,
but not resentment.

Power can overcome power,
but not empower.

Bombing can end a war,
but not build peace.

Killing can turn another person to ashes,
but what rises from ashes?

Blessed are the peacemakers,
for they will be called children
of God ■ Matthew 5:9

six

Loving

I am the vine, and my Father is the vine-grower...this is my commandment that you love one another as I have loved you.

■ John 15:1, 12

You shall love the Lord your God with all your heart, and with all your soul, and with all your mind. This is the first and the greatest commandment. And the second is like it: You shall love your neighbor as yourself.   ■ Matthew 22:37–39

Love can be more far reaching when it is holistic and fertile. That is why Jesus uses the image of the vine and branches. Love is about being rooted and at home with our families and human communities, but it is also about being at home with our mother the earth. Love, like a vine, is meant to branch out. But we cannot love to the fullest degree, unless we are at home with self at the deepest level of our spiritual lives. Spiritual health at our deepest core enables and empowers our loving. From that inner core we can connect over and over again with a wider circle of life. And it is this expanding circle of love that has the power to ultimately withstand all dangers and terrors.

Our Spiritual Health

I remember a wintry Saturday in February when I was a pastor of a parish in Omaha. Actually, the weather was more than wintry, it was nasty. A combination of snow and sleet the night before had left the parking lot a mish mash of slush and ice. As I crossed the lot I noticed a young child, nine or ten years old, going into the church by himself. I was curious about him being up so early and coming to the Saturday Mass alone. I knew he was not an altar server. So after Mass, I stepped over to the pew where he was huddled. As I came up to him, I realized he was shivering. Then I noticed what he was wearing—a flimsy football jersey. He had sloppy and totally wet shoes with no socks! We had a long talk and I discovered that he had slept the night before in a laundromat. He was sockless and at this moment homeless. Being homeless is also being rootless. No vine can flourish when uprooted. We found a home for him at Boys Town—now renamed Girls and Boys Town—where he experienced an expanding circle of love and an opportunity for developing a holistic spiritual life.

Father Val Peter, the director of Father Flanagan's famous Girls and Boys Town, continues to welcome young people who have been bruised and scarred—some even terrorized by stressful environments. They are in need of a home, of love, and of spiritual health. And Father Flanagan's home has had phenomenal success in fostering spiritual health in family cottages and through a holistic approach to living. Father Peter describes that spiritual health process in his book, *Rekindling the Fire*.

Spiritual health is interconnected with your entire life…Spiritual health...is the interface of physical (exercise, eating healthy foods, managing stress), the social/emotional (building friendships, giving service, listening empathetically, creating energy), the mental (reading, visualizing, planning, writing, developing talents, learning new skills), and the spiritual (meditating, praying, practicing the...works of mercy, reading the Scriptures, reconnecting to following the Lord.

The whole purpose of the holistic process of growing in love that Father Peter describes is to enable the citizens of Father Flanagan's home to love God with all their minds and hearts and souls and their neighbor as themselves. It is the fulfillment of the Great Commandment. From that core of fulfillment, healthy love radiates outward.

But what of those who are confined at home by sickness, those who suffer, those in care centers? How is their love to radiate out? It can—for they are powerhouses of prayer. Although confined, their prayer, no matter how feeble, can reach out and touch the world. I recently visited Bob Andahl, retired from the Air Force, now confined to a chair in his living room, but who used to take Meals-on-Wheels to shut-ins. Now his only wheels are on his chair. Around him are machines. Twice his breathing apparatus began to beep, and unless tended, he would quickly suffocate. No complaints ever. No undue anxiety. After he had been re-attached to his ventilator, his wife, Pat, remarked—"You know, he is the prayer leader around here. He keeps us all praying."

The Hyper Pace of Modern Life
Stephan Bertman, writing in "The Futurist," reflects on this rushed hyper pace of modern life. He says that as the velocity of our everyday life increases—we fly faster and faster through the atmosphere of daily experience and encounter a turbulence our bodies were never designed to withstand. Robert Reich, in his book *The Future of Success*, reports that in the new century Americans work harder and longer hours than any people of any other developed country. To attain spiritual health, or to even have much time to concentrate on love or loving in these circumstances, is almost impossible. He reports that when the economy is in bloom, some people make a lot of money but keep running faster

because they do not know what tomorrow will bring. Others run faster just to keep up. And when economic recession occurs, the wealthiest lose their dividends and the rest lose their jobs. So in both cases there is anxiety and stress.

Excessive and unrelenting stress is the "masked and hidden terrorist" stalking our lives. The weapons of stress are heart attacks, cancer, and strokes. Smoking is just as much a terrorist threat as someone who would send you an envelope full of anthrax. The only difference is that it kills in a slower fashion.

So what personal spiritual resources can we draw upon in the face of danger or disease? How are we to have peaceful and loving hearts—rather than exhausted and endangered ones? Perhaps considering the very word "disease" might be a good starting point. Dis-ease literally means not being at ease, being off balance. Since we live in a topsy-turvy world, trying to find balance is a difficult quest. Imbalance is very dangerous for our holistic well-being. The following suggestions could all be called spiritual disciplines because when we take care of ourselves we are reverencing the body/spirit God has given us. We take care of ourselves so that we can love God and neighbor. It all fits together.

The Importance of Prayer
Find cracks in the midst of each day to insert prayer. Pauses in the whirlwind can be energizing. Pray at stoplights for the persons ahead of you. Pray on the elevator for those around you. Pray at your desk at the start of your work or when you wait for the computer to boot up. Make a list of people who need your prayers and mention them daily to God. You will be plugging into the great powerhouse of universal prayer. At some time in the day, relax and just calm your breath and join it to the calmness of the Holy Spirit. Slow down for a minute or two and concentrate on your breathing. Clear your mind. Richard McBrien writes that "silence is one of the most durable forms of prayer in the lives of individual people of faith." Even if the bathroom is your only place of silence, pray there.

Sometimes take a slow bath instead of a quick shower and imagine that you are immersed in the love of God. Shut out sounds and totally relax. Just be loved by God. Thomas Merton writes that contemplative prayer is about "resting in God." How much of a chance do you give God to nourish and love you? One of the primal discernment questions of the human is: "Am I lovable?" God says "Yes!" Listen to God's affirmation.

Reverence Earth

Tests have shown that patients who have hospital windows that look out on nature heal quicker than those whose windows look out at brick walls. Also people who are prayed for recover sooner! Since most of us live in cities far from the great outdoors, we need to be creative in finding ways to be in touch with nature. As I write this, I can look up from the screen at a picture of a brook cascading down a mountainside. If I look to the right of my desk I can gaze on a blue fish swimming about under the canopy of a growing green plant. I also have a beautiful scene on the screen saver of my laptop. Such things nourish our souls. Saint Teresa of Avila, who reformed the Carmelite order and went about establishing new convents, demanded two prerequisites for such convents. They were to be poor, and they were to have a garden!

Part of reverencing earth is to reverence water. Meditate before it sometimes and recognize its beauty whether it is in a fish bowl or fountain or even in your bath. See it as something you depend on for life. When Jesus wanted to describe spiritual effervescence, he promised "a fountain of water springing up to eternal life." About water, one physician remarked: "If we drank twice as much water, we would have half as much sickness!"

Move Away from Worry and Self-Pity

When we were children we worried about passing tests. When we were teens, we worried about being accepted. When we were young adults, we worried about finding a mate, and on and on it went. Now we worry about terror. If we were to collect all these worries, put them in a bag, and throw them overboard, we would not miss any one of them! It is like the albatross in Coleridge's *The Rime of the Ancient Mariner*:

> The self-same moment I could pray
> And from my neck so free
> The albatross fell off, and sank
> Like lead into the sea.

Try to replace your worries with laughter. We all need some sort of "laugh oasis" that we can depend on for regular doses of laughter. For me, it is the sitcom "Everybody Loves Raymond." Find yours. Some physicians have found a correlation between heart disease and laughter—the more the laughter, the better for your heart.

Treasure Each Day

There is a great surge of energy when we move forward. There is a great depletion of energy when we look back with regret or when we feel sorry for ourselves. The cliché "Today is the first day of the rest of your life" is still very true. What counts is now. So treasure the moment you have rather than worrying over what might happen. Treasure your work, too, and consider it a spiritual discipline. Alert yourself that your work and interactions at work are spiritual disciplines. Bless your work and offer it for the glory of God. When I was a high school student, we were told to put the initials "AMDG" at the top of all papers. I still do every day that I write. It means "All For The Glory Of God." There is a beautiful saying in Ireland when two workers meet: "God bless the work!" The response is "And God bless you too!" Greg Pierce, in his splendid book, *Spirituality@Work*, reminds laypersons that "Work is all the effort (paid or unpaid) we exert to make the world a better place, a little closer to the way God would have things." This kind of work is the path of holiness for most people!

Be Present to Others

Take time to share the joy of others, to make friends, and to strengthen relationships. "Where your treasure is, there is your heart." Recognize that your loved ones and your friends are your priceless treasures.

If we love ourselves, we cannot abuse ourselves. Addictive substances suck the very source of life from us. Yet for many people, when addictions are at their worst, they are closest to God's help! The 12-step path to recovery used by Alcoholics Anonymous has helped countless people to love God and themselves. And recovery is the best way to love themselves and those closest to them.

Be Proactive about Anxiety

Writing in September of 2000, a year before the terrorist attacks, Mary Ellen Lernter wrote, "Anxiety is America's No. 1 health problem!" She said that anxiety affects 19 million people each year. The World Health Organization reports that anxiety disorders doubled in the last four decades of the twentieth century. In working with youth at Father Flanagan's home, Father Peter has found many entering the home beset with anxiety—unable in their own lives to control the unpredictable, and as a result, deeply anxious. The new century is unpredictable no matter how much we want everything under control. A holistic spirituality, rooted in our trust in God, is the best way to deal with our anxiety. (Of course, when anxiety or depression becomes clinical, seeking medical help is important.)

Dr. Thomas McCauley of Scottsdale, Arizona, after over 40 years of treating illness, believes that excessive stress is at the root of most illnesses. Make a list of your major stresses. Can some be eliminated? Can some be lessened? Then make a list of your greatest stress reducers. See if they are getting the attention they deserve.

Consider the Larger Picture

Fear of terrorism and other overt dangers might well obscure and narrow our vision and we might miss a far larger menace—a creeping terror and danger that daily grows more lethal. When this enemy approaches, we might well say, "We have met the enemy and it is us!" This "terrible thing" that we all are involved in is the devastation of our earth home! We cannot live a holistic lifestyle or spiritual life and at the same time be alienated from our earth home.

In his book *The Dream of the Earth*, geologian Thomas Berry writes about our polluting the air with acids, the rivers with sewage, the seas with oil—all of this is a kind of intoxication with our power to devastate in an order beyond reckoning. This is the terror our lifestyles bring to our earth home. Thomas Berry goes on to say:

If we were truly involved by the beauty of the world around us, we would honor the earth in a profound way...and turn away with a certain horror from all those activities that violate the integrity of the planet. That we have not done so reveals that a disturbance exists at a more basic level of consciousness and on a greater order of magnitude than we dare admit to ourselves or even think about.

Instead of "turning away with horror," we inflict horror on the earth in thousands of unreflective ways. When we fail in our love for the earth we fail to love our children and grandchildren for we bequeath to them a poisoned legacy. Every fiber of their bodies comes from earth. If we curse the earth, we curse our children! At Assisi, honoring St. Francis as a patron of ecology, Pope John Paul addressed this issue in very strong words, saying that we have a "grave responsibility to preserve the order in the universe...for future generations." And then for greater emphasis, he said, "I repeat that the ecological crisis is a moral issue." Loving the earth, then, is a moral imperative.

To live full and peaceful lives, even in the shadow of danger or ter- ror, we need to believe that we are rooted in our earth home and in Christ. He is the vine and we are the branches. Christ the vine was root- ed in earth. No particle in his body came from heaven. His body came from fertile, crop-producing earth! To lead full spiritual lives we need to love the earth where we are rooted, and recognize Jesus as the Lord of heaven and earth. We also need to love our neighbor as ourselves and to let our love radiate outward in the concentric circles of family, neighborhood, city, state, nation, and world community. And this will enable us to love God with our whole minds, our whole hearts and our whole souls.

Journal Questions

- "I am the vine. You are the branches." What does this statement from Jesus mean to me personally?
- What part does prayer play in my life? What part would I like it to play?
- How do I handle stress and anxiety?
- What does it mean to me to "honor the earth"?

Origins

Dear child,
I want to share with you your origin
and your destiny.
You came from love.
Like the sea rushing to the shore,
tides of love brought mom and dad
together.
You were conceived in love,
held safe in love,
brought to life through love.
I want you to grow
in a circle of love.
Your circle will widen,
but the core of your circle
is always safe and secure.
You are connected by love,
connected by care,
connected by understanding,
and connected to God,
your origin and your destiny.

seven

Parenting

The most important ingredient to recovery from any trauma is to remain connected with other people.

■ Sandra Bloom, Psychiatrist

She was a very young mother. He was older. Their whole relationship got off to a rocky start. She was pregnant before the nuptials. The neighbors whispered and talked. But she was the love of his life and he tried to avoid their skeptical eyes and prying nosiness. He kept himself busy with his work. He was not only a working man but also a dreamer. Sometimes he dreamed of cabinet designs and new ideas for chairs. He was very good at working with wood. But sometimes he had other dreams and he trusted his dreams. His dreams always told him that things would work out.

Their child was a boy and he was born in terrible times amid great danger. There was a terrorist with great power who was out to kill children. So the early years were tough. They even had to flee to escape this terrorist threat. Finally things settled down. They were able to return to their home. The father had enough work to keep him busy and even set some aside for a pilgrimage, which was half vacation and half prayer. When their vacation weekend finally arrived, they set out on their journey with other relatives and friends. This was a happy group headed up to the capital, somewhat like happy folks on their way to a football stadium on a crisp October Saturday. There was prayer at holy places but also camaraderie and reunion of relatives. Their son ran and skipped and frolicked with many of his cousins. Sometimes he and his cousins would run off and not be seen for an hour or so and as mothers did then and still do today, after a while, his mother would wonder where he was. But then, she would say to herself, "Well, he is thirteen now and I guess we have to cut him a little slack now and then." However, when he returned laughing and smiling with his cousins, she would smile with relief.

Finally, it was time for the whole pilgrimage group to head home. They stretched out in a long line as they walked toward home. They felt fulfilled, full of the happy glow that comes when relatives come together to celebrate life and faith. It was only later that she turned to her husband and said, "Who is our son with?" and he, startled, replied, "I thought you knew!" Now they looked into each other's eyes and saw the shadow of fear.

So what had happened? He, like many young teenagers before him and after his time, was pushing the boundaries, testing the reins, and he had set out on an adventure of his own. So his parents went back to the city and searched for him with increasing alarm. Finally, to their great relief, they found him. And we are told that Jesus returned home with them and grew in age, wisdom, and grace.

Unhappy Searches

Sadly, missing children stories too often do not have happy endings. Not too far from where I live, two pre-teen girls heard the bell of an ice-cream truck as it passed by. They went out on the porch and saw that it had stopped at the next block. It was daylight so they felt safe jumping on their bikes and riding down to the next block. When they arrived, the younger girl realized she did not have enough money, so she got on her bike and raced home for some more money. When she returned a few minutes later, the ice-cream truck was gone and so was her sister. Only her bicycle lay by the roadside. She was never found.

Being a parent is one of the great joys of life but it carries with it a fear for the safety of children. Added to the ordinary fears of this kind, parents now—especially since September 11—must be alert for danger from other sources. To be vigilant yet not obsessed, to be concerned but not unduly worried, requires a balancing act between denial of danger and panic.

Gleanings from Children
Following the terrorist attacks, I went to youth workers and mentors and listened to what they had to say. I also asked children to write out how they felt about this tragedy. Here are some of the thoughts and feelings of grade school children—most from ten- and eleven-year-olds in that betwixt and between time of growth.

The terrorists want us to be frightened and not safe. They are somewhat like bullies. (a girl)

The terrorist attack has affected my life by being scared to fly. My parents and teachers have helped me by showing me that not everything will be the same again, but our lives will be close to the same as before the attack. (a boy)

The impact of the September 11 attack "hit" me hard. But the teachers said, "Don't be afraid," and so did my dad. The teachers helped by talking about it and my parents helped by reassuring me. I know, though, that God will help us to get through it. (a boy)

I know my folks occasionally talk about it. I felt shock. But I want to put my focus on school, sports, animals, and still be alert at the same time. I am concerned about biological and chemical warfare. (a girl)

Some ask, "Where was God?" I think God was all over. He held the towers up long enough for some people to get out. Yet for some, it was their time to be with God. Even though I'm really sad, I think with help from my family and close friends we can make it. We will stand strong and be ready for the next thing that may come. (a girl)

The terrorist attacks had no effect on me at all. I have trust in God that he will keep me safe. If I do get hurt or die, I know I will go to heaven because I am a good person. Heaven will be OK too because it is supposed to be beautiful and wonderful. My parents and teachers are affected and they keep telling me that everything will be fine. But deep in my heart, I already know that. Everything WILL be all right as long as we have faith in God. (a girl)

I was having a very horrible day when my mom came in and told me what happened. Later our teachers and parents let us express our feelings. I liked that. Even today, I am still wondering about what is going to happen next, but that is something only God can answer. (a girl)

The terrorist attacks just brought us together like never before. Why? Their goal was to scare us. It didn't work. We are united as one. My teachers and parents have been very understanding when we talk about the tragedy. If it weren't for them, I do not know what I would do. (a boy)

These are but a few samples from many. One common theme that ran through almost all of the responses was that parents and teachers are listened to maybe more than they give themselves credit for. And they are observed. The way parents act, their behavior, is even more important than words. Behavior makes a big impact in either lessening or increasing anxiety in children.

Gleanings from Parents and Educators
So what did some wise and experienced parents and educators do and say in the wake of tragedy? And what do parents need to do to calm the

fears of children? The responses I got from teachers and other mentors could be summarized as follows: Seize the moment! When any tragedy strikes, take it as a unique opportunity to listen to children and empathize with their feelings. Also, genuine play is an antidote to anxiety, so play with children and laugh with them. Computers, video games, and mechanized toys cannot replace the human presence of parents, nor can they replace the joy of human interaction.

> If you were ever to watch so closely,
> you would observe play
> as a primal blessing.
> Take time to watch a lamb skipping
> or a young colt frolicking.
> Take time to watch a child skipping down the street.
> No one taught them—no one coached them.
> Skipping must be deep down in our DNA.
> For it is the rollicking rhythm of primal play!

When was the last time…you played jump rope with your children? Or plopped yourself down on the floor and played a game with your grandchildren? For many adults in America, carving out time to play during the busy day—whether weekday or weekend—is often a memory of times past. Children's lives mirror those of adults. Perhaps our overscheduled Type A Society is beginning to reach a saturation point and is saying, "Enough is enough." ■ *National Toy Association 2001–2002 Fact Book*

Remember that adult behavior has more impact on children than words, so try to keep your own anxieties in check. Those who lead in a nurturing, strong, confident, and warm way succeed in making their children feel secure. For a child, the central question is: "Are my parents in charge? Are my parents in control?" At the same time it's important to monitor TV and computer use so that children aren't exposed to situations and opinions they can't handle. To illustrate this there is a story about a teacher telling the story of Jonah to a second-grade class. After the story, the teacher asked the children what they would do if they were Jonah.

They all raised their hands, as they always do at that age, even when they don't have an answer. But when the teacher recognized a little girl, the tot replied, "I'd call my dad, and he would get me out!" Little ones need to be assured that their parents will always love and protect them.

Sister Eileen Marie, a long time educator with fifty years of experience, said, "Parents should ask themselves, what is the most important room in the home for the family? And what goes on there?" Is it interactive and alive, or a dull, passive place where only the TV reigns? "Parents must see their home as a house of affirmation where they welcome, embrace, trust, and affirm."

Pray daily with your children. Daily prayer is a way for parents to calm the fears of their children. When children are invited to pray, they vocalize their hopes and wishes, and this kind of prayer empowers and assures them.

A second-grade teacher told me: "In the shadow of a disaster, I think the children I teach want to know if they are OK. I had second graders who could not sleep after seeing only a minute of horrible destruction on TV. We talked more with them about their feelings than the incidents themselves—and being able to verbalize fears helped children cope with them."

Further Implications

Tragedy, whether national or personal, is a unique opportunity for parents to spend some quality time with their children. Children are like a plowed field, ready for planting. When weeds of fear and terror have been planted, seeds of consolation and confidence must be planted too. As time goes on, the weeds can be "pulled" through ongoing dialogue. When traumatic events occur, parents should be prepared to spend more time than usual with their children.

I spoke with Mary whose parents went through the horrors of the Second World War. Listening to their vivid stories of death and horror had a tremendous impact on her. Now she realizes that she suffered from post-traumatic stress way into her high school years. When children hear and see horrible stories, they need to be listened to and their feelings honored.

This is especially true today when the threat of terrorism is so present. This new moment has changed our social climate. A precocious fifth grader who had gone through a lot of personal trauma in his family acknowledged this same change. When asked about the terrorist attacks, he replied, "I just used to be a freaking anarchist. Nothing was valuable to me. But when I saw those firemen going into that tower—I changed my mind. There are some things that are valuable."

Recently I invited seventh graders to write a newspaper column, either about what parents need to know in troublesome times, or what gives each of these children hope. Katie Kiefer wrote the following advice to parents and kids as Ann Landers or Dear Abby might:

In Troubled Times
To all you kids out there:
"Talk to your parents. You need to find answers. Don't try to figure them out on your own."
To all you parents out there:
"Your kids need you right now and not later. This is a great time to spend more time together. It's called 'becoming a family.' Be strong and don't show them you're scared.
You gotta be the grown-up. Become closer to your kids. Spend time with them. Be their parents. They love you."

When tragedy strikes, or in troubling times, parents need to seize that unique moment to listen to and empathize with their children, and, of course, they need to affirm them, encourage them, reassure them, and then do it some more.

Journal Questions

- How have I handled the attacks of September 11 so far with my children? How have they responded?
- In what ways have I tried to help my children feel secure?
- When was the last time I genuinely played with my children, or laughed with them? How might I find more time for this in the future?
- In what times and situations can I pray with my children? What forms might our prayer take?

Saint Paul's Letter to the Corinthians
(through a child's eyes)

My mom and dad are patient.

My mom and dad are kind.

They are not jealous or rude.

My mother and dad are not quick tempered or angry.

They do not brood over injury.

There is no limit to their ability

To forgive and reconcile.

They say, "I am sorry."

My mother and dad believe that

There are three things that last:

Faith, Hope, and Love

And the greatest of these is love.

> *Love of God.*
>
> *Love of Family.*
>
> *Love of one another.*

■ Sister Patricia Marie Stack,
Scottsdale, Arizona

eight

Praying

The prayers, sayings, and reflections in this chapter are meant to give voice to the feelings all of us have experienced in the shadow of terror, danger, and anxiety. My hope is that these prayers will inspire you to pray in your own voice and with your spouse, children, friends, and coworkers.

The student asked the master: "What does hope do?'

The Master replied: Hope pushes. Hope pulls. Hope lifts up. Hope moves. Hope looks ahead. Hope vaults. Hope bounces. Hope skips. Hope dances. Hope gets up. Hope reaches out. Hope stretches. Hope consoles. Hope enables. Hope empowers. Hope energizes. Hope inspires. Hope waits. Hope endures. Hope springs eternal.

The student asked the Master: "Is hope always on the move?"

"No," replied the Master, "Sometimes hope rests like an anchor in the depths of our souls."

Prayer for Hope

O God when I need to endure, give me hope.
When I need to move, give me hope.
And when I cannot move, let my soul be at peace,
anchored by hope in the depths of my soul.

Deepening Prayer

Sit upright in a straight but relaxed posture. Take some moments of
quiet to relax and quiet down. Began to shut off noises and the inner
static of the high paced and racing thoughts that fill your head. When
you reach a point of inner and outer quiet, notice your breathing in
and out. Just stay with your concentration on your breathing. Then, as
you begin to breathe out, say in your mind: "Jesus." That is your
prayer—just repeating the name "Jesus" with every exhalation. When
distracting thought patterns intrude, just gently re-focus and continue
breathing and exclaiming: "Jesus."

Crying Out to God

How long, O God?
I cry out for help but you do not listen!
I cry out to you, "Violence!"
But you do not intervene.
Why do you let me see ruin;
why must I look at Misery?
Destruction and violence are before me;
there is strife and clamorous discord.
Then God answered and said:
Write down the vision clearly upon the tablets
so that one can read easily.
For the vision still has its time,
presses to fulfillment and will not disappoint:
If it delays, wait for it
it will surely come; it will not be late.
The rash one has no integrity;
but the just one, because of faith shall live. ■ Habakkuk 1:2–3;2:2–4

Psalm 10

Wake up Adonai! O God lift up your hand!
Don't forget those who are helpless!
Why do the violent renounce you, God?
Why do they say in their hearts,
"You won't call me to account?"

But you do see;
you see every trouble, every cause for grief;
you ponder it and take it into your hand.
The helpless commit themselves to you;
you are the helper of the orphan.
Break the arm of the violent and the evildoer!
Seek out corruption till you find no more!

You will rule forever and ever, Adonai,
and those who do not acknowledge you
will perish from the land.
Adonai, you hear the desires of the meek;
you strengthen their hearts
and bend your ear to them,
to do justice for the orphan and the oppressed
so that those born of earth may strike terror no more.

Peace Prayer of St. Francis

Lord, make me an instrument of your peace. Where there is hatred,
let me sow love; where there is injury, pardon; where there is doubt,
faith; where there is despair, hope; where there is darkness, light; and
where there is sadness, joy.

O Divine Master, grant that I may not so much seek to be consoled
as to console, to be understood as to understand, to be loved as to
love. For it is in giving that we receive; it is in pardoning that we are
pardoned, and it is in dying that we are born to eternal life.

Prayer for Those Going into Battle

O God, as we battle, let our cause be just. We raise our shields against
terror. We gird ourselves with courage. We seek neither empire nor
domination. May our arms bring only liberation.

Send Saint Joan of Arc to ride with us. Send Angel Raphael to wres-
tle evil. Send Saint Peregrine to tend to wounds. Send Angel Michael
with the golden shield so our spirits facing terror never yield.

When the battle's over, guns are stilled, may dreams of peace be fulfilled. May love be planted in bloody sand. Let us bind up wounds and
honor dead. May the hard won victory perish dread. Remember these
for whom I pray: (recite names).

Lead Kindly Light

Lead kindly light, amid the encircling gloom,
Lead thou me on;
The night is dark, and I am far from home,
Lead thou me on.
Keep thou my feet; I do not ask to see
The distant scene; one step enough for me.

■ John Henry Cardinal Newman

Prayer of Saint Teresa of Avila

Let nothing disturb you,
Nothing give you fright.
All things are passing;
God alone unchanging,
Endure patiently.
Attend to all things.
Who God possesses
Nothing is wanting.
God alone is enough.

Saint Patrick's Lorica: The Deer's Cry

Morning Prayer, Part 1

I arise today through God's strength to pilot me; God's might to uphold me, God's wisdom to guide me, God's eye to look before me, God's ear to hear me, God's word to speak for me, God's hand to guard me, God's way to lie before me, God's host to save me from snares of devils, from temptations of vices, from everyone who shall wish me ill, afar and anear, alone and in multitude.

Part 2
Christ to shield me today against poison, against burning, against drowning, against wounding, so that there may come to me abundance of reward. Christ with me, Christ before me, Christ behind me, Christ in me, Christ beneath me, Christ above me, Christ on my right, Christ on my left, Christ when I lie down, Christ when I sit down, Christ when I arise, Christ in the heart of everyone who speaks of me, Christ in every eye that sees me, Christ in every ear that hears me.

I arise today, through a mighty strength, the invocation of the Trinity, through belief in the threeness, through confession of the oneness, of the Creator of Creation.

For Those in the Service
Jesus, you served your disciples with the generous wine of Cana. With the great gift of healing, you served the centurion in charge of many troops. There are other centurions, people "in the service." Their service stands between our peace and looming terror, our homes and toxic horror. *Semper fidelis*, sentinels—in the air, on the ground, over the sea, and under the sea. No greater love than this, you said, than to lay down their lives for their friends. Bless these servants; gird them with honor.

For Public Servants
Do you know what I have done to you? You call me teacher and Lord— and you are right, for that is what I am. So if I, your Lord and Teacher, have washed your feet, you also ought to wash one another's feet.

■ John 13:12–14

Prayer For Fire and Rescue Workers
O God, at the sound of a bell they come, riding red multi-horse wagons, coats flapping in the wind. They are a comrade band—these fire

quenchers. The fires of hell would not deter them. They ride to help, to save, to battle the fires. St Florian, their patron, ride with them. Protect them and bring them safely home.

Prayer For Police and Law Enforcers
They are a thin blue line, these servants of the law. They defend the battleground between chaos and order, 'tween agents of evil—and the common good. Saint Michael the Archangel, defend them in battle. Protect them from the snares of the enemy. Saint Raphael, ride with them and bring them safely home.

Prayer at Moments of Crisis and Decision Making
There is a tide in the affairs of men, which, taken at its flood, leads on to fortune; omitted, all the voyage of their life is bound in shallows and in miseries. On such a full sea we are now afloat; and we must take the current when it serves, or lose our ventures.

■ William Shakespeare, *Julius Caesar*

Silent Reflection
O God, at this moment of crisis and this moment of decision, help us to seize the moment. Grant the grace of discernment so that we might "take the current" and run with the noblest tide.

The Terror of Serious Illness
I pray for those at war with sickness. Cancer sneaks in a hidden foe; Alzheimer's a smokescreen; strokes like mortar fire. Illness is an enemy needing to be scouted, needing to be discovered, needing to be routed out. I pray for these sick ones: (recite names). Gird them for battle, and grant them courage. Give them the inner peace to marshal all resources: prayer, good care, compassion all around.

Prayer to Saint Peregrine, Patron of Cancer Sufferers
Loving God, in spite of all that you give to us, we still find suffering in our lives. You generously offered healing to our brother Peregrine. Following his example, we turn to you with our troubles.

Strengthen those who suffer from cancer and other serous diseases.

Look kindly upon us all and heal us. Give life to our bodies that our lives might be long and happy. Give us comfort in the troublesome moments of our personal lives. Heal us of hurt and resentment. Give grace and joy to our spirit, that we may continue to praise you. We ask this through Christ, our Lord.

■ from Servants of Mary St. Peregrine Shrine, Omaha, Nebraska

Anima Christi
Soul of Christ make me holy.
Body of Christ, save me.
Blood of Christ, fill me with love.
Water from Christ's side wash me.
Passion of Christ, strengthen me.
Good Jesus hear me.
Within your wounds, hide me.
Never let me be parted from you.
From the evil enemy, protect me.
At the hour of my death, call me.
And tell me to come to you.
That with your saints I may praise you.
Through all eternity. Amen.

Morning Prayer
O God, come to my assistance. O God make haste to help us. I thank you for this new day, for every sunrise is gift. I offer all that I do today for your greater honor and glory. Glory be to the Father and to the Son and to the Holy Spirit.

Father, through your divine grace, I am growing in the Spirit and on the path the Spirit leads me. I am walking a blessing path. I am growing in love. Blessed be! Blessed be!

Guardian Angel Prayer
Angel of God, my guardian dear, to whom God's love commits me here. Ever this day be at my side to light and guard, to rule and guide. Amen.

Night Prayer

Now fades away the sun of day. Now cease the toil, and pray. Now comes the cloak of darkest night to cover over stress and fright. Send your holy angel from heaven O God, to watch over, to cherish, to protect, and to bless all who dwell in this house.

O God, I pause to ask forgiveness for any thing offensive in my life today....O God, I pause to remember those for whom I want to pray....

Mary Prayer

Hail, Mary!
Black shadows,
Like spilled ink
Upon parchment
Cover over
Words, questions
Exclamations.

Day's events
All rolled up
Into the night.
Night chanting
From distant ages:
Salve Regina!

Mary's cloak
Enfold us.
Jesus' shroud
Surround us.
Holy Spirit bless
The cave of
dreams.

O God, grant us a
peaceful night
and a perfect end.
Amen.

■ Hymn from *A Contemporary Celtic Prayerbook*,
ACTA Publications